1

Hi, I'm Uncle Ken Jones. Today, we're going to talk about seaweed. I've been a fisherman for most of my life. These days, I talk to people about Caring for Country. One of the most important things in the ocean is seaweed, or kelp.

Knowledge Books and Software

3

Australia has the most types of
seaweed in the world. Many are
found nowhere else in the world.
The Limestone Coast off South
Australia is a "seaweed hotspot".
The main reason for this is because
it has cool, clean water.

Knowledge Books and Software

You can find seaweed in many different colours and shapes. Brown kelp has kelp bubbles that you can eat. The fluffy, soft seaweed that washes up on the beach can also be eaten. It can be cooked or eaten raw in salads.

Knowledge Books and Software

7

Bull kelp is the biggest and strongest type of kelp. It is attached to the ocean floor by its roots. A long tail grows up from the roots. The seaweed grows out of this. It floats to the surface to get the sunlight it needs to survive.

9

Bull kelp grows in "forests". It gives shelter to many types of fish. It's also a hunting ground for seals. It can drag flint and pebbles to the shore to make new landforms. The flint has been used to make tools by First Nations people for many years.

Knowledge Books and Software

For thousands of years, the First Nations people have been great fishermen. They dive into the water and swim through the seaweed. They find crayfish along rock ledges. They also find other fish that are hiding in the kelp.

Knowledge Books and Software

During high tides, the bull kelp is pushed further up the beach. It makes a rich compost for the plants growing in the dunes. Many people also collect this seaweed for their garden. It helps their plants to grow.

When the seaweed breaks down, it brings many insects. These insects become food for many birds. This helps them to fly a long way back to where they came from.

Knowledge Books and Software

First Nations people used to make boots from bull kelp. The long, flat strips were shaped into walking boots. They were lined with possum fur. These boots made it much easier for them to walk long distances when trading.

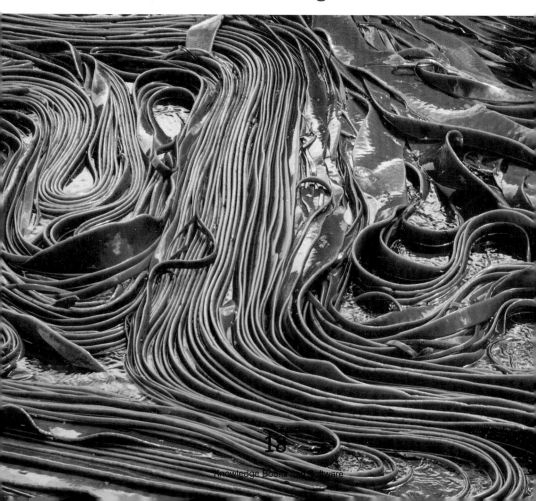

19

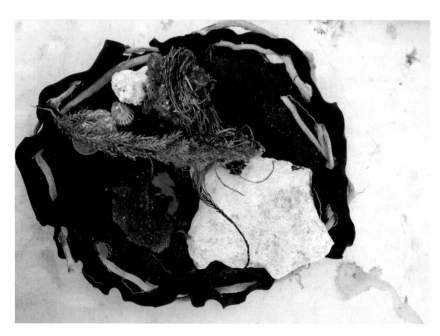

Another smart idea was the "seaweed esky". Bull kelp was cut and shaped. It was then lined with wet sea feathers. Fresh crayfish could then be carried a long way and kept cool. Crayfish were then traded for things like spears and boomerangs.

Knowledge Books and Software

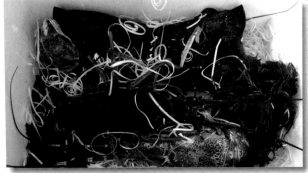

Seaweed has helped to keep the oceans healthy for thousands of years. Without it, the whole coast would be out of balance. Our First Nations people knew this. Caring for Country has helped to keep this balance. First Nations Elders are now sharing their knowledge with scientists to help discover new uses for seaweed!

Knowledge Books and Software

23

Word bank

important

ocean

Australia

Limestone

different

attached

surface

landforms

thousands

crayfish

compost

collect

esky

boomerangs

balance

knowledge

scientists

Knowledge Books and Software